The Murders At Convict Lake

by George Williams III

illustrated by Dave Comstock

TBR Trust
P.O. Box 20703-CL
Carson City, Nevada 89721
To order books visit our web site:
www.Autographed-Books.com
or call 1-775-750-8646

Published by:
TBR Trust
web site: **www.Autographed-Books.com**
P.O. Box 20703-CL
Carson City, Nevada 89721
e mail: gjw@aol.com
phone/fax 1(775)750-8646

Non-fiction books by George Williams III:

Rosa May: The Search For A Mining Camp Legend (1979)
The Guide to Bodie and Eastern Sierra Historic Sites (1982)
The Redlight Ladies of Virginia City, Nevada (1984)
The Murders at Convict Lake (1984)
The Songwriter's Demo Manual and Success Guide (2000)
Mark Twain: His Life In Virginia City, Nevada (1986)
Mark Twain: His Adventures at Aurora and Mono Lake (1987)
Mark Twain and the Jumping Frog of Calaveras County (1999)
Hot Springs of the Eastern Sierra (1988 revised 2002)
On the Road with Mark Twain in California and Nevada (1995)
In the Last of the Wild West (1992, revised 1994 and 1999)
Hot Springs of Nevada (1996)
Hot Springs of Northern California (1998 revised 2002)

Library of Congress Cataloging-in-Publication Data

Williams, George, III, 1949-
The murders at Convict Lake.
1. Murder--California--Mono County--History--19th century--Case studies. 2. Nevada State Penitentiary--History--19th century--Case studies. 3. Escapes--History --19th century--Case studies. I. Title.
HV6533.C2W54 1984 364.1'523'0979448 83-18116
ISBN 0-935174-11-7 (PBK.)

Printed in the United States of America by American Craftsmen

Author's Introduction

The following story should be of particular interest to Californians and Nevadans. In fact anyone interested in the Wild West of the 1870's should find the story interesting. It has all the drama of a great western motion picture and it's all true. There are sheriffs and posses, outlaws and gunfights and yes, even a hanging.

In 1871, twenty-nine of the West's worst characters--murderers, rapists, train robbers, and horse thieves, escaped from the Nevada State Penitentiary in Carson City. Six convicts made it as far south as Mono County, California where they killed two men beside a lake in Long Valley near Bishop. Today this lake is known as Convict Lake.

Since that time, many details have been distorted. Some writers created huge posses of 300 or more men. The names of the murdered victims were changed. Important characters and incidents were neglected.

To discover what really happened, I went back to the newspapers of the day: the Carson Daily Register and Bishop's Inyo Independent. County and state records were used to corroborate newspaper accounts.

Using old maps and U.S.G.S. topographic maps, I retraced the route taken by the convicts as they fled from Carson City to Bishop where they were captured. Then I drove and at times hiked the route. Using the maps and illustrations provided, you too can retrace the convict's escape route. It's fun, interesting and helps you to feel a part of the pursuing posse.

I hope you will enjoy reading THE MURDERS AT CONVICT LAKE. I enjoyed researching the story and writing it. If you have any questions or would just like to write, feel free. I'd like to hear from you. Enjoy.

George Williams III
Benton Crossing
Long Valley, California
August, 1983

mailing address:
Box 413
Riverside, CA 92502

TWENTY-NINE CONVICTS ESCAPE FROM THE NEVADA STATE PENITENTIARY

Sunday evening, September 17, 1871, twenty-nine of the West's most desperate outlaws busted out of the Nevada State Penitentiary at Carson City. Six made their way into Mono and Inyo counties, California where they murdered three men. Of these six convicts, five were caught and two of them hung near Bishop, California.

Carson City today is the Nevada state capital. The pleasant town lies at the north end of the high Carson Valley nearly surrounded by mountains. To the west is the Sierra range, to the east the Pine Nut Mountains and to the north the barren Washoes. It is a thirty minute drive to Reno or Tahoe. As in times past, Carson City is on a highly traveled route for those heading to Reno, Tahoe, Sacramento or Los Angeles.

Carson City grew naturally. Western travelers camped there before crossing the Sierra during and after the California gold rush. There was water, the Carson River, a mile and a half east of town and several hot springs whose baths soothed the weary traveler. In 1859 when silver and gold were discovered in Gold Canyon ten miles northeast of Carson, the great Comstock boomed and Carson became a freighting hub and train connection for travelers heading to and from San Francisco.

Designated as Nevada's capital in 1862, Carson City became the site of the Nevada State Penitentiary. In 1860, Abe Curry built the Warm Springs Hotel at Warm Springs, a mile and a half east of town on Fifth Street, less than a mile west of the Carson River. In 1862, the state leased the hotel to hold prisoners. This building was destroyed by fire in 1867. A stone prison was later constructed with rock from a nearby quarry. Another Warm Springs Hotel was built next to the prison and served as a resort.

In the beginning, the Lt. Governor presided as prison warden. In September, 1871, Lt. Governor John Franklin "Frank" Denver, after whose brother Denver, Colorado was named, served as prison warden. Frank Denver lived in a small apartment within the prison with his wife Mary, and their six year old daughter, Jennie. Bob Dedman, a life term prisoner, worked for the Denvers as servant and waiter.

Denver's apartment was on the ground floor. In the second story there were bedrooms. Deputy Warden Zimmerman also had a bedroom in the second story. Next to Zimmerman's bedroom, there was a small storeroom where rifles and ammunition were kept. Above the bedrooms and

Panorama of Carson City about 1870. Nevada Historical Society.

the storeroom was the prison attic, large enough for men to crawl through.

For weeks preceding the uprising, there were rumors of upcoming trouble. It had been a long, hot summer. The prisoners were more restless than usual. The guards' morale was down. The rumors were not taken seriously by Denver and no precautions were taken.

Sunday, September 17, an easterly wind blew down from the Sierra full and hard and turned the Carson Valley into a dust bowl. Sundays were usually quiet at the prison. Only one guard, Volney Rollins, was on duty inside the prison. While Frank and Mary Denver entertained friends at dinner, Volney Rollins let the prisoners out of their cells to enter the large room adjoining the cells where the six o'clock meal was served.

After the prisoners finished eating, Rollins entered the large room to lock up the prisoners for the evening. Then it began.

In the preceding weeks, the prisoners had prepared themselves for the break. They had made sling shots, knives and sewn pieces of metal into their cuffs.

As Volney Rollins entered the large room, a prisoner struck him behind the head. Rollins fell. As the prisoners attacked him, Pat Hurley, a prisoner, grabbed Rollins by the collar and dragged him into a cell and locked the door.

The Nevada State Penitentiary in the 1870's. Nevada Historical Society.

Below, Warm Springs Hotel. Matt Pixley was killed on the porch to the left. Nevada State Museum.

The prisoners climbed on top of their cells and cut a large hole through the plaster and lath ceiling leading to the attic. One by one the prisoners climbed into the attic and silently made their way through the garret. Above Zimmerman's bedroom, they cut a hole in the ceiling unaware Zimmerman was asleep in the room below.

There was a great noise as the prisoners crashed through the bedroom ceiling. Zimmerman, startled, awoke and fled downstairs. The convicts quickly broke through the plaster and lath wall into the storeroom and stole several weapons and ammunition.

At first, Denver and his guests thought the crash was an earthquake. Then Zimmerman rushed downstairs and warned them of the break.

As the convicts poured down the stairs toward Denver's apartment, Frank Denver, derringer in hand, flew into the stairwell to meet them. Bob Dedman, the lifer, followed Denver. As Denver entered the stairwell, Frank Clifford, a 29 year old horse thief in for ten years and apparent leader of the break, led the mob. Denver shot Clifford in the abdomen then rushed into his room for his 6 shooter and returned to the fight. Though stunned, Clifford and other convicts rushed Denver. One convict struck Denver in the back of the head with a sharp metal object. Another hit him

Frank Denver met the convicts as they came down the stairs.

in the forehead with a sling shot making a gash 3½ inches long. As Denver went down, Leander Morton grabbed his gun and shot him as he lay on the floor. Bob Dedman grabbed a chair and swung it at the convicts felling five and knocking one down the stairs. Dedman was eventually knocked senseless and left for dead.

Led by the wounded Clifford, the prisoners climbed down the stairs and seized the armory and ammunition. The prisoners now were armed with 3 Henry rifles, 4 double barreled shot guns, several 5 and 6 shooters and 2500-3000 rounds of ammunition.

Being Sunday and the prisoners usually locked up, there were no guards on the outer wall. Those guards on hand were outside the prison.

F.M. Isaacs, a guard from Gold Hill was in the yard with a 6 shooter when the prisoners came out. Isaacs began firing but was shortly hit with a bullet that passed through his right knee, broke it, and lodged in the rear of his left knee. Isaacs shifted his weight to his left leg and continued firing until he was shot in the hip and went down.

John Newhouse, a guard, then fired at the prisoners. He shot E.B. Parsons, a Verdi train robber, and several prisoners before he was shot in the back of the head. He fell, wounded but alive.

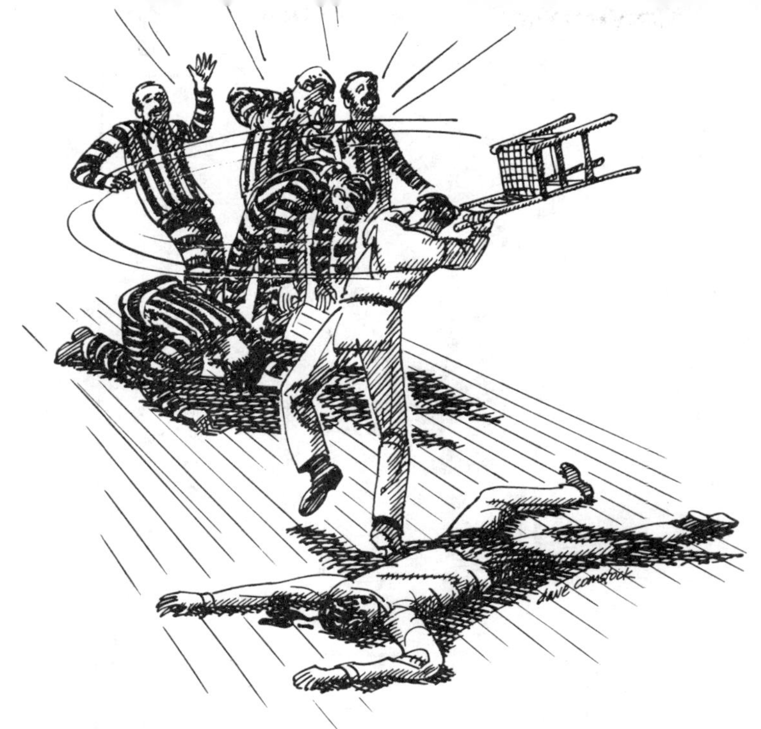

Bob Dedman, the lifer, fought to save Denver's life.

Then Perasich, an unarmed guard, ran into the Warm Springs Hotel, grabbed a 5 shooter and began shooting at the escaping mob. Perasich hit three prisoners before he was shot in the hip, the bullet passing into his groin and lodging half way down the thigh between the femeral artery and the bone. He was left helpless near the prison door.

Along with Perasich, Matt Pixley, the young proprietor of the Warm Springs Hotel, rushed into the yard firing at the prisoners who were still in the prison guard room. Pixley rushed the guard room and fired through the window. Charlie Jones, a 22 year old murderer, shot Pixley just below the left eye and through the head. Pixley fell on the stone porch, dead.

A French guard, Henry, fired several shots into the mob until his gun emptied. Then he fought the prisoners bare handed until they were outside the yard.

In the midst of the shooting, Denver's 6 year old daughter, Jennie, became frightened and ran into the yard where the shooting was taking place. Seeing the doomed little girl, Ed Goyette, a prisoner, rushed into the yard and pulled the child to safety. Later he helped "Burgie", Pixley's bartender, drag the wounded Isaacs to safety. Burgie convinced Goyette he would be killed for his heroic actions if he returned to the prisoners. Goyette allowed

Matt Pixley was shot and killed by Charlie Jones.

Burgie to lock him in a hotel room until the shooting was over.

Henry Phillips was at the Warm Springs Hotel in a buggy. When the shooting began he rushed to town and warned Sheriff Swift of the break.

Sheriff Swift and twelve to fifteen armed riders started out immediately but arrived too late. Of the twenty-nine escapees, twenty-two marched off, two a breast, headed east over the high ridge beyond the prison, then turned south and followed around the ridge. Two convicts passed through the southern portion of Carson and five headed northeast across the railroad between Carson and Empire, a suburb northeast of Carson where mills were located.

Clifford and Parsons were believed to have been shot. Eight to ten others were also believed wounded. The prisoners had carried their wounded off.

Dr. Lee and Dr. Waters rushed to the prison to help the injured. Frank Denver was shot in the hip. The bullet had passed up the hip ten inches and had lodged near the spine. Dr. Waters dressed Perasich's wound but was unable to find the bullet. It was necessary to amputate Isaacs' left leg. He would die within a month from his wounds.

The saving of Jennie Denver by prisoner Goyette. Below, F.M. Isaacs firing at the convicts as they entered the yard.

The pursuit begins

Governor Lewis Bradley was not in Carson at the time of the prison break. Charles Belknap, his Private Secretary, took charge. At 7:00 PM Belknap telegraphed General Batterman at Virginia City and asked that he organize the militia and come immediately. Batterman arrived three hours later by special train with twenty-seven National Guardsmen and Lt. James Lyman with fifteen of the Emmet Guard.

At 10:30 PM Deputy Sheriff Gus Lewis and six men rushed to Genoa to warn citizens of the prison break.

At 12:30 AM, Monday, September 18, Lt. Hyman and Tom Harkin, Storey County Deputy Sheriff and eleven men, began to pursue the prisoners, six and a half hours after the break.

At 1:30 AM General Batterman, thirteen guardsmen and a few citizens followed Lt. Lyman's posse until daylight then scoured the willows along the river as they headed back toward the prison.

At 9:00 AM Sheriff Swift, Sheriff Atkinson of Storey County, Chief of Police George Downey, detective Ben Lackey, an Indian guide and eight men followed the convicts' trail from the prison wall down to the river. A half mile below the Mexican dam, about two and a half miles from the prison, the convicts had crossed the river. A half mile up the hill beyond the river, they had split up. Eight went up the river, eight down and the remaining thirteen headed south toward Pine Nut Valley.

Swift followed the main body of thirteen toward Pine Nut Valley. Through the sand hills the posse tracked the convicts easily and kept a steady pace but along the rocky ridges they went slowly.

At Pine Nut Valley, Sheriff Swift found an old charcoal maker, a Dutchman, tied up. The Dutchman had been robbed by six convicts. One of them was called Burke. The convicts had three Henry rifles, one double-barrelled shotgun and one or two six shooters. They had stolen the Dutchman's four horses, ransacked three nearby cabins and stolen provisions. Apparently the thirteen convicts had divided near Pine Nut, the six robbing the Dutchman.

These six convicts would eventually flee more than 200 miles into Mono and Inyo counties, California. There they would murder three men. Two convicts would be hung, one barely escape hanging and two others escape a lynching in Aurora.

The six convicts were Charlie Jones, John Burke, Tilton Cockerill, J. Bedford Roberts, Moses Black and Leander Morton.

Upper left, Gov. Lewis Bradley, absent when the prison break took place. Right, Charles Belknap, Bradley's private secretary who took charge. Middle, Frank Denver, prison warden. Below, the Verdi train robbers and lawmen. Tilton Cockerill, one of the six convicts is shown. Also shown are Police Chief George Downey and detective Ben Lackey.

Charlie Jones, 22, had been sent up for stabbing a man through the heart in a fight near Hamilton. Jones was 5' 10" with brilliant hazel eyes, light brown hair and small ears. He was wiry and athletic.

The Dutchman referred to a man called Burke. This was John Burke. He was 23 and had been convicted of manslaughter and jail breaking. Burke was 5'8", 150 pounds, a Texan, fair skinned, blue eyed, dimpled chin, nervous, intelligent and perceptive.

Tilton Cockerill, 37, had been a miner before he was sentenced to 23 years for robbing a train at Verdi near Reno.

J. Bedford Roberts, 18, was the youngest. He had been sentenced to 11 years for stage robbery. He was 5' 7", 122 pounds, dark brown hair, large brownish-grey eyes, small head, thin face, large nose and thin compressed lips. Roberts was thought to be from Long Valley where the convicts would first be cornered.

Moses Black, 34, was in for seven years for grand larceny. He was large and heavy with dark hair and beard. He had only been in prison six days at the time of the break.

Leander Morton, 27, was a small man. He had been sentenced to 30 years for mail robbery. Morton was extremely dangerous.

Charlie Jones had worked as a teamster in Esmeralda county, Nevada and in Inyo and Mono counties, California, and knew tne country as far south as Los Angeles. John Burke knew the country as well. Roberts, supposedly from Long Valley, surely knew the country as far south as Bishop. While retracing the route the six convicts took into Mono and Inyo counties, it was very apparent that someone in the party knew where he was going and knew how to get there. The land of the 200 mile route is harsh and waterless for long stretches. Knowing where hidden springs were located helped the convicts tremendously.

From Pine Nut, the six convicts headed east across the rough Pine Nut Mountains. Sheriff Swift's Indian guide followed the the convicts' trail until after dark when the posse reached a rocky ridge making it impossible to follow their trail further. The Indian scanned the distant mountains and pointed to a peak 3 or 4 miles away. He told Sheriff Swift there was a spring there and he believed the convicts went there. The whites in the posse disagreed and were reluctant to cross the valley of brush and rocks in the dark. Swift thought the Indian was right and ordered the posse forward. The posse crossed the valley, climbed the rugged peak and camped beside the spring. In the morning

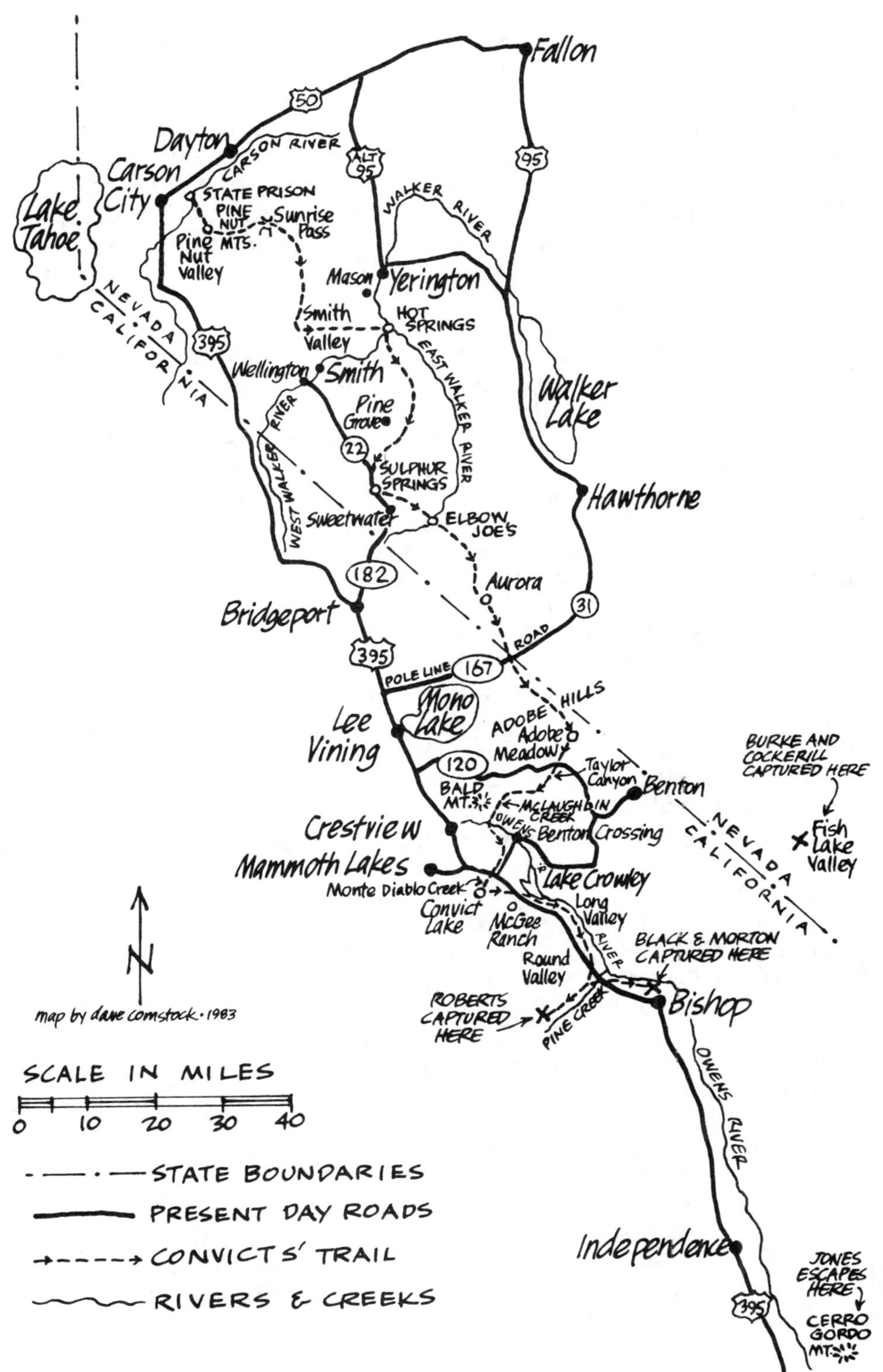

Fallon
50
Dayton
Carson City
Lake Tahoe
CARSON RIVER
ALT 95
95
STATE PRISON
PINE NUT MTS.
Sunrise Pass
Pine Nut Valley
WALKER RIVER
Mason
Yerington
NEVADA
CALIFORNIA
Smith Valley
HOT SPRINGS
395
Wellington
Smith
EAST WALKER RIVER
Walker Lake
WEST WALKER RIVER
Pine Grove
22
SULPHUR SPRINGS
Hawthorne
Sweetwater
ELBOW JOE'S
182
Aurora
Bridgeport
31
ROAD
395
POLE LINE
167
ADOBE HILLS
Mono Lake
Lee Vining
Adobe Meadow
120
Taylor Canyon
Benton
BURKE AND COCKERILL CAPTURED HERE
BALD MT.
McLAUGHLIN CREEK
Crestview
OWENS
Benton Crossing
NEVADA
CALIFORNIA
Fish Lake Valley
Mammoth Lakes
Lake Crowley
Monte Diablo Creek
Convict Lake
McGee Ranch
Long Valley
RIVER
BLACK & MORTON CAPTURED HERE
Round Valley
ROBERTS CAPTURED HERE
PINE CREEK
Bishop
N
map by dave comstock · 1983
SCALE IN MILES
0
10
20
30
40
OWENS RIVER
STATE BOUNDARIES
PRESENT DAY ROADS
CONVICTS' TRAIL
RIVERS & CREEKS
Independence
395
JONES ESCAPES HERE
CERRO GORDO MT.

the posse found the convicts' trail not ten steps from the spring. The Indian estimated they were six hours behind the convicts.

The convicts crossed the Pine Nut Mountains at Sunrise Pass and headed into Smith Valley late Monday night. At 1:00 AM Tuesday, September 19, the convicts reached Hot Springs on the Walker River, 10 miles north of Wellington on the Dayton road. They rested at Hot Springs. Knowing the road to Aurora would be heavily traveled, the convicts headed north and then east of Pine Grove, a mining camp. They then headed southwest and struck the Aurora road between Wellington and Sweetwater near Sulphur Springs.

Sheriff Swift and his Indian guide trailed the convicts to Hot Springs. There their horses gave out and they were forced to turn back. The posse was still six hours behind the convicts. Sheriff Atkinson of Storey County, Chief of Police, Downey, detective Ben Lackey and eight others continued the chase through Tuesday.

Billy Wilson operated the pony express from Aurora to Carson City. At 1:00 PM Tuesday afternoon, Billy Poor, an 18 year old kid from Aurora, left Sweetwater for Wellington on his first mail ride for Billy Wilson. Thirty hours later Poor had not arrived at Wellington, 22 miles away. Wilson feared the rider had been waylaid by the convicts.

Tuesday afternoon, September 19, the posse headed by Sheriff Atkinson gave up the chase. Only the angry Dutchman continued the pursuit hoping to catch up with the convicts and retrieve his horses.

At 2:00 AM Wednesday morning, September 20, the six convicts passed Elbow Joe's on the Walker River, 17 miles north of Aurora.

By noon Wednesday, Wilson's pony rider still had not reached Wellington and a rider was sent south to look for him. Near Sweetwater the rider found the convicts' trail. The convicts now had five horses, the addition likely being Poor's horse. The worse was feared for young Billy Poor.

Early Wednesday morning, the six convicts passed near Aurora heading south. Billy Poor was believed to be with them. Charles Belknap received a wire from John Wheeler in Aurora who claimed he knew where the convicts were and would pursue them.

Later Wednesday, the convicts stopped at George Hightower's sawmill near Benton. Charlie Jones, the murderer, dressed in Billy Poor's coat and boots, asked for salt and flour. Jones claimed to have a party of miners in the woods. One of the six was barefoot and was believed to be Billy Poor.

At 9:00 PM Wednesday evening, the Aurora posse began

to pursue the six convicts. The posse was made up of Horace Poor, Billy's father, Deputy Sheriff Palmer, J.S. Mooney, P. Kelly, Ned Barker, John McCue and a man called Lewis.

The Aurora Posse trailed the convicts to Adobe Meadows where they made camp. In the morning an Indian told the posse that six men were camped 5 miles up the canyon.

By this time, the Aurora posse was fatigued and some men were sick. Horace poor begged the men to go forward but only J.S. Mooney was willing.

Thursday, September 21, Deputy Sheriff Palmer decided to turn the chase over to Deputy Sheriff George Hightower of Benton. He wrote Hightower a note explaining that six convicts were in his area. The convicts were believed to have Billy Poor with them for protection. Hightower should be careful not to shoot the boy.

Palmer explained that his men were tired and sick. A reward of $500 each was offered by Nevada for the capture of the convicts--dead or alive. He urged Hightower to act quickly. Palmer sent the not to Benton by messenger.

That evening, Henry Devine and McLaughlin left Benton for Adobe Meadows, 17 miles distant. In the morning they were joined by the rest of the Benton posse, George Hightower, Robert Morrison, a 34 year old Wells Fargo agent and soon to be married, J.C. Calhoun, B.B. Alonson, James and George Dougherty, I. Nabors, James Peregrine, Nesbitt and Moore. In Long Valley, Alpers would join the posse.

At 2:00 PM Friday, September 23, the Benton posse started up Taylor canyon following the convicts' trail. They

The convicts crossed Adobe Valley toward Taylor Canyon near Long Valley.

crossed the mountains at McLaughlin Creek and went 18 miles into Long Valley.

The six convicts continued south along the Aurora to Owens River Road. They crossed today's Pole Line Road north of Mono Lake, went east of Mono Lake through the pumice sand and then across the Adobe Hills. They crossed Adobe Valley, full of sagebrush and blooming yellow rabbit brush, as they headed toward Bald Mountain. Fourteen miles west of Benton they crossed today's Highway 120, went through Adobe Meadows and followed the old Aurora to Owens River Road up Taylor Canyon toward the head of McLaughlin Creek.

In the meadows at the head of McLaughlin Creek, the convicts looked across Long Valley and saw the looming Sierra range. They must have believed, once across the Sierra, they would be free. They might have succeeded if not for a cold blooded murder committed by Carlie Jones and Leander Morton.

The six convicts near Long Valley

Friday morning, September 22, the convicts descended McLaughlin Creek Canyon following the old wagon road beside the creek. Sagebrush, wild rose bushes, bitter

The trailer to the right sits in Adobe Meadows where the Benton posse picked up the convicts' trail.

brush and snow berry bushes were all about them. At the foot of McLaughlin Creek, they crossed the shallow Owens River, then climbed up the basalt bluff. Then they went east around the timber and headed south through the sagebrush hills 6 miles toward Monte Diablo Creek at the foot of the Sierra.

Friday evening, the Benton posse caught up with the convicts at the foot of the Sierra. Robert Morrison spotted the convicts near what was then called Monte Diablo Creek, today called Convict Creek. The Hightower posse decided to spend the night at Alney McGee's ranch at McGee Creek, 3 miles south and confront the convicts in the morning.

The shootout

Saturday morning, September 23, the convicts awoke hungry. Jones, Burke and Cockerill took a cup and went up Monte Diablo Canyon toward the lake in search of berries. They were gone an hour before the Benton posse surprised Morton, Black and Roberts at their camp in the lower canyon.

The Hightower posse went up Monte Diablo Creek. As the posse neared the narrow eastern end of the deep cup where Convict Lake lies, they spotted a man running down a hill 100 yards ahead. The posse spurred their horses and

Aurora and Owens River Road historical marker placed by E. Clampus Vitus on Highway 120, 14 miles west of Benton at Taylor Canyon.

The old Aurora and Owens River Road as it heads down McLaughlin Creek Canyon, discovered by the author.

were soon within 40 feet of the convicts' camp. Morton, Black and Roberts hid behind a large pine tree on the south side of the stream and began firing. They killed two of the posse's horses and wounded two others. One of the posse was shot through the hand.

Convicts Black and Morton did all the shooting. In the first fire, Roberts, the boy convict, went into the open and was shot in the shoulder and foot. Roberts managed to crawl to the tree where Morton and Black hid. Morton said to Roberts, "Get into the willows. They will surround us here and I will be shot."

At the first rounds of fire, the entire posse except for Robert Morrison, retreated to the willows. Morrison crawled down the canyon trying to get closer to the convicts. Black and Morton spotted Morrison. "There's a brave chap. I don't want to kill him," Black said. "That's the kind to kill. Then you won't have any trouble with the cowards," Morton said. Black then started to cut off Morrison but passed him up. Morrison spotted Black and pulled his trigger. His pistol cap exploded but the gun did not fire. Black wheeled and shot Morrison in the side. Morrison fell, wounded but alive. Black went over to Morrison. Morrison raised up partially and tried to steady his hand to shoot Black but he was too weak. Black coolly pointed his gun at the back of Morrison's head and fired. The bullet passed through Morrison's head and out just above the right eye,

Black coolly walked up to Morrison and shot him through the head.

killing him instantly.

Morton and Black then collected five pistols left behind by the posse as they fled. The posse also left several horses which Morton, Black and Roberts rode up the canyon.

They soon came upon Mono Jim, an Indian who had been told to hold his and Hightower's horse. Jim thought the three men were members of the posse and called out to them. When he realized his error he started running crying out in a whining tone. Black shot him. Lying on his side, Jim managed to shoot Black and Morton's horses. Then Morton shot Mono Jim through the eye and took his horse.

It is not known how Jones, Burke and Cockerill escaped. Jones evidently later split from Cockerill and Burke. He was never seen after the Monte Diablo shootout. Burke and Cockerill were later captured in Fish Lake Valley, on the east side of the White Mountains.

Morton, Black and Roberts fled south through Long Valley and down the old road into Round Valley, north of Bishop.

In the evening, Alney McGee recovered the bodies of Robert Morrison and Mono Jim. Mono Jim was buried in the canyon where he was killed. Morrison was taken to Benton and buried in the Masonic Cemetery. Today the tallest peak above Convict Lake is called Mount Morrison. The lake and the stream have since been known as "Convict."

This stone building was Robert Morrison's Wells Fargo Express office in the 1870's. Today it is the Benton General store. Below, the grave of Robert Morrison in the Benton cemetery.

The grave of Deputy Sheriff George Hightower whose posse first cornered the convicts at Monte Diablo. Below, the graveyard at Smith, Nevada, where Billy Poor is buried in an unmarked grave.

Morton, Black and Roberts reach Bishop

Word was sent by messenger from Benton to Bishop that the three convicts were in the Bishop area. A posse was formed in Bishop led by John Crough and John Clark. The Bishop posse picked up the convicts' trail in Round Valley.

Hoping to finally cross the Sierra and reach freedom, the convicts climbed Pine Creek Canyon near Round Valley. The climb was steep and difficult. They abandoned one horse and lost another over a cliff.

Sunday, September 24, the three convicts ate their last food.

The Bishop posse finally located the convicts in Round Valley. Fearing the convicts' superior Henry rifles, the posse sent I.P. Yaney for help to the military post in Independence, 60 miles south. Major Harry Egbert and five men hurried to Bishop in seven hours. Egbert carried a large supply of arms for any citizen who joined the posse.

The capture of Morton and Black

Wednesday night, September 27, ten days after their escape, Leander Morton and Moses Black were captured in the sand hills 5 miles southeast of Round Valley. They were taken by J.L.C. Sherwin, Hubbard, Armstead, McLeod and two Indians. A few shots were fired before Morton and Black threw up their hands and surrendered. An Indian misunderstood this action and shot Black through the left temple and head but did not kill him. Morton and Black were taken to Bircham's, a homestead in Round Valley.

Strangely, Black was conscious and able to talk. Morton claimed young Bedford Roberts had killed Morrison. Hearing Morton's story, the posse resumed the hunt for Roberts in Pine Creek Canyon.

Friday, September 29, the posse was eating lunch in Pine Creek Canyon when there was a movement in the willows within twenty yards of them. They ordered Roberts to come out and surrender. Roberts did so. He was wounded in the shoulder and foot from the shootout at Monte Diablo Creek. He had been left behind by Morton and Black because he was wounded and couldn't travel. Roberts said it would be alright if they killed him if he could just have a cup of coffee. He hadn't eaten for 5½ days.

Roberts was taken to Bircham's. When Morton was confronted by Roberts, it was obvious to the posse that Morton and Black, not Roberts, had killed Morrison and Mono Jim.

Roberts confessed that Charlie Jones and Leander Morton

killed Billy Poor near Sulphur Springs, between Sweetwater and Wellington.

Roberts told the gruesome story of Billy Poor's murder. Near Sulphur Springs, Morton sent Roberts ahead to learn if a nearby milk ranch was run by a single man or a family. If it was run by a single man, Morton wanted to kill him to prevent him from telling the authorities that they had passed by. Morton didn't want to kill a family man or a family. After tying up the Dutchman, Morton told the others they should kill any man they came upon. This would protect them. Charlie Jones agreed to do the killing with Morton.

Roberts was at the milk ranch stealing potatoes from a field, when Billy Poor rode by, going south. Shortly after he heard two shots.

When Roberts returned to the others, Morton and Jones were wearing citizens clothing. When he asked Jones where he got his clothes, Jones joked. Jones later said it had been a mistake capturing the pony rider. They at first intended only to use him for protection but things got out of hand.

Morton and Jones were expecting to meet a Captain Dingman riding the pony. Dingman had been a guard at the prison and had killed several convicts in an earlier escape attempt. Morton and Jones wanted to kill Dingman.

When Morton and Jones stopped Billy Poor, they asked about Dingman. Poor said he would be down on the next day's stage. Jones said they want to "cook Dingman's goose."

"You son-of-a-bitch," Morton said. "You've let the cat out of the bag." Fearing Poor would tell others their plans, Morton and Jones pulled the rider from his horse. Billy Poor begged them not to kill him but later Jones bragged, "We didn't give him much time to beg, did we, eh Morton?"

Both Jones and Morton shot Billy Poor, stole his clothes and boots and dressed him as a convict. They took two rings from his hands. Jones bragged that he would "wear his ring to hell." Then they burned Poor's head. "They'll think he's some poor convict son-of-a-bitch," Morton said.

A little ways from Sulphur Springs, they passed the milk ranch. Jones wanted to kill the rancher and throw his body into the cellar but Burke said, "I don't go a cent on such cold blooded murders as that. We will have the whole country after us. I am going to leave this crowd. I'll take my rifle and horse."

"Oh no you won't," Morton said.

"If any of you bother me I'll shoot out your guts," Burke fired back. "There's no use in this," Cockerill said. Burke then said to Morton, "You couldn't kill him [Billy Poor] with one shot. You had to shoot him twice." Morton and Jones still wanted to kill the rancher but Burke continued his protest and prevented them.

Men were sent from Wellington to Sulphur Springs, 15 miles south of Wellington. Billy Poor's body was found a half mile below Sulphur Springs, 200 yards west of the road. He had been shot in the head. Poor's body was taken to Wellington and his father and mother were notified in Aurora.

You can find Sulphur Springs in Dalzell Canyon in the Toiyabe National Forest, about 9 miles north of Sweetwater Ranch on Highway 182. Today an old stone cabin rests beneath the cottonwoods at Sulphur Springs. The springs are $\frac{1}{4}$ mile north of the cabin, 300 yards west of the highway in a 12 foot gully. Magpies, blackbirds and sandpipers call from the willows beyond the muddy meadow.

Charlie Jones and Leander Morton killed Billy Poor, the pony rider, at Sulphur Springs.

Lynched, tried and hung

Sunday evening, October 1, Morton, Black and Roberts were placed in a wagon. With a guard of horsemen, the Bishop citizens started for Carson City to return the convicts. Near Pinchower's store where the northern road through West Bishop intersects the main drive, the wagon and horsemen were suddenly surrounded by a large body of armed vigilantes.

"Who is the captain of the guard," a vigilante asked.

"I am. Turn to the left and go," but the mob did not move. Silently and without resistance, the guards gave up their prisoners to the vigilantes.

Roberts was afraid of what was to befall and protested going with the vigilantes. Morton knew it was inevitable. Sitting beside the driver he said, "Give me the reins and I'll drive after them. I'm a pretty good driver myself." The wagon followed the vigilantes across an unfenced meadow to a vacant cabin a mile northeast. Black and Roberts, both wounded, were carried into the cabin. Morton walked by himself.

The cabin was lighted and the trial began. The convicts were questioned for two hours and afterwards votes were taken for each prisoner. The jury agreed Morton and Black were guilty and should be hung at once. J. Bedford Roberts, the boy stage robber, received equal votes and was saved.

A scaffold was quickly built. One end of the beam rested on the top of the chimney while the other end was supported by a tripod of timbers.

Morton heard them building the scaffold and asked, "Black, are you ready to die?"

"No, this is not the crowd that will hang us."

"Yes it is. Don't you hear them building the scaffold?" Then Morton turned to Roberts and said, "We are to swing and I mean to have you swing with us if we can. We want company."

The hanging

Men carried Black out and lifted him into the wagon below the scaffold. After he was raised to his feet he stood unsupported.

Morton walked out by himself, calmly looked over the sight, climbed aboard the wagon and placed the noose over his own head. "Please tie my hands so I can't jump and catch the rope," he said. This was done. Black asked for water.

"Do you have anything to say," someone asked.

"No," Black said.

"It isn't right for a man to be hung without some kind of religious ceremony. If there's a minister here, I'd like to have a prayer," Morton said. Strangely, a minister was among the vigilantes. He stepped forward and spoke a few words.

Morton said, "I am prepared to meet my God--but I don't know that there is any God." Morton shook hands with the men in the wagon. The minister prayed. Black sighed. As "Amen" was said, the wagon moved slowly away. Black, large and heavy, died without struggle. Morton, sprang into the air but did not move a muscle after his weight rested on the rope.

The hanging of Morton and Black.

End of the trail

On October 5, through the help of Mary Denver, Bob Dedman, the lifer who had heroically defended Frank Denver, was pardoned.

October 6, Chat. Roberts, father of J. Bedford Roberts, learned that his son was still alive. F.M. Isaacs, the wounded prison guard, nears death.

October 7, Charlie Jones is reportedly found dead in an abandoned cabin in Fish Lake Valley, murdered by Burke and Cockerill. The five convicts were angry at Jones. Before his hanging, Morton confessed that he, Black, Roberts, Cockerill and Burke had followed Jones blindly into Mono and Inyo counties. Jones supposedly knew the area and claimed to have friends who would help them. But it was Jones' cold blooded murder of Billy Poor that had incensed the Mono people and sent a posse down their necks. Morton moaned about the "hornets nest" Jones had led them into.

The report of Jones' death proved untrue. He was last seen crossing the Cerro Gordo mountains into Death Valley.

He was never captured.

October 11, John Burke and Tilton Cockerill were delivered to the U.S. Deputy Marshall in Carson. Both were charged with the murder of a United States mail carrier--Billy Poor--and the robbing of mail by force of arms. Burke and Cockerill had been captured in Fish Lake Valley by John Helm, Esmeralda County Sheriff, John Wheeler, John Ludwig and another man. The prisoners were brought to Aurora after their capture. There Sheriff Helm and others were offered $500 if they would leave the jail for a few moments.

October 12, J. Bedford Roberts was moved from Bishop to Camp Independence for protection by military guard.

October 13, F.M. Isaacs, 39, dies.

October 14, the coroner's jury finds the twenty-nine convicts responsible for Isaac's death.

October 27, J. Bedford Roberts is returned to the Nevada State Penitentiary.

Eighteen convicts are tried for murder

By November 15, eighteen of the twenty-nine escaped convicts had been captured. Two had been hung and nine others including Jones were still at large.

November 15, the eighteen convicts are indicted for the murder of Isaacs. Afterwards they are arraigned for the murder of Matt Pixley.

November 21, the trial for Isaac's murder begins. It lasts one week. On November 28, the jury finds all eighteen convicts not guilty. Testimonies show that most of the shooting was done by Jones and Morton. Jones was blamed for the deaths of Matt Pixley and Billy Poor, and Morton for the murder of Isaacs and Billy Poor.

J. Bedford Roberts' conviction for stage robbery was appealed to the Nevada Supreme Court on grounds that he had not received a fair trial. Roberts won his appeal and was released from prison in 1873.

The 1871 prison break created much controversy over the way the Nevada State Penitentiary was run. Soon after, the Nevada Legislature voted to appoint a full time professional warden.

Frank Denver unwillingly gave up his position as warden. He died in San Francisco August 12, 1875 and was buried in the Lone Mountain Cemetery in Carson City.

Order these books personally autographed and inscribed by George Williams III.
Or visit our web site to order
www.Autographed-Books.com
Or Call 1-775-750-8646 for more information.

NEW! HOT SPRINGS OF NORTHERN CALIFORNIA Leads you to more than 45 hot springs between Bishop California and the Oregon border. Accurate road directions, photos, maps and George's "2 cents." 88 pages, $12.95 Quality paper.

NEW! HOT SPRINGS OF NEVADA George's brand new book lists more than 40 hot springs all over the state of Nevada. As always, George gives accurate road directions to each hot spring, a photograph of each hot spring and George's "2 cents." 72 pages. AUTOGRAPHED. Quality paper $10.95

3rd revised edition HOT SPRINGS OF THE EASTERN SIERRA 80 pages. AUTOGRAPHED. $10.95 Quality paper..

NEW! IN THE LAST OF THE WILD WEST The true story of the author's attempt to expose the murders of prostitutes and corruption in Virginia City, Storey County, Nevada, home of the largest legal brothel in the United States. 272 pages. AUTOGRAPHED. $12.95.

ROSA MAY: THE SEARCH FOR A MINING CAMP LEGEND Virginia city, Carson City and Bodie, California were towns Rosa May worked as a prostitute and madam 1873-1912. 30 rare photos, 26 personal letters. 240 pages. AUTOGRAPHED. $10.95 quality paper..

THE REDLIGHT LADIES OF VIRGINIA CITY, NEVADA Virginia City was the richest mining camp in the American West. From 1860-95, Virginia City had three of the largest redlight districts in America. Perhaps the best and most informative book on prostitution in the old West. Plenty of historic photos, illustrations, map and letters. 48 pages. AUTOGRAPHED. $6.95 quality paperback; hard cover, $10.95.

THE GUIDE TO BODIE AND EASTERN SIERRA HISTORIC SITES True story of the rise and fall of Bodie, California's most famous mining camp, today a ghost town, National Historic Site and California State Park. Known as the toughest gold mining town in the West where millions were made in a few years, murders were a daily occurrence. Has a beautiful full color cover with 100 photos on an 8 1/2 X 11 format. 88 pages. AUTOGRAPHED. $12.95 quality paperback.

THE MURDERS AT CONVICT LAKE True story of the infamous 1871 Nevada State Penitentiary break in which 29 outlaws escaped and fled more than 250 miles into Mono and Inyo counties, California. They vowed to kill anyone who got in their way. In a terrible shootout at Monte Diablo, today known as Convict Lake just south of Mammoth Lakes ski resort, the convicts killed two men.. 18 rare photographs 32 pages. AUTOGRAPHED. $5.95 quality paperback..

MARK TWAIN: HIS ADVENTURES AT AURORA AND MONO LAKE When Sam Clemens arrived in Nevada in 1861, he wanted to get rich quick. He tried silver mining at Aurora, Nevada near Mono Lake not far from Yosemite National Park. Clemens didn't strike it rich but his hard luck mining days led to his literary career. 32 rare photos, mining deeds and maps to places where Clemens lived, wrote and camped. 100 pages. AUTOGRAPHED. $8.95 Quality paperback..

MARK TWAIN: HIS LIFE IN VIRGINIA CITY, NEVADA While reporting for the *Territorial Enterprise* in Virginia City, 1862-64, Sam Clemens adopted his well known pen name, Mark Twain. Here is the lively account of Mark Twain's early writing days in the most exciting town in the American West. Over 60 rare photos, maps to places Twain lived and wrote. 208 pages. AUTOGRAPHED. $10.95.

Mark Twain and the Jumping Frog of Calaveras County The true story of Twain's discovery of "The Celebrated Jumping Frog of Calaveras County," the publication of which launched his international career.. 116 pages, index, bibliography, 35 photos, guide maps for travelers. AUTOGRAPHED. Quality paper $8.95.

New ! On the Road with Mark Twain in California and Nevada A handy guide to Mark Twain's haunts in California and Nevada 1861-68. Road directions to historic sites, guide maps, 100 photos. A must-have book for Twain fans who would follow his trail in the far West. 136 pages, 100 photos, road maps, index. S16.95 Quality paper; $29.95 hard cover. AUTOGRAPHED.

THE SONGWRITER'S DEMO MANUAL AND SUCCESS GUIDE shows the songwriter and aspiring group how to make a professional demo tape at home or in the studio and how to use it to sell songs and land record deals. Williams explains how the music business operates, who the important people are and how to make contact with them. Illustrations and complete resource Appendix. $16.95 PAP.; $29.95 AUTOGRAPHED.

REPAIR YOUR CREDIT. Everything you need to know to clean up your bad credit and build good credit. Contains all the form letters to use to contact the credit reporting bureaus. By following the instructions in this book, you should be able to clean up your bad credit within in six months and begin to obtain credit cards. $16.95 three-ring binder with forms.

Order Form

Name____
Address________________________________City______________
State_________________________Zip____________________
E-Mail address_______Yes, George, please send me the following books personally autographed and inscribed by you:

___Copy (ies) Hot Springs of Northern California, $12.95 paper.
___Copy (ies) Hot Springs of Nevada, $10.95 paper.
___Copy (ies)Hot Springs of the Eastern Sierra; $10.95 paper.
___Copy (ies) In the Last of the Wild West, $12.95 paper
___Copy (ies) Rosa May: The Search For A Mining Camp Legend, $10.95 paper.
___Copy (ies)The Redlight Ladies of Virginia City, $6.95 pap.
___Copy (ies)The Guide to Bodie, $12.95 paper.
___Copy (ies)The Murders at Convict Lake, $5.95 paper.
___Copy (ies)Mark Twain: His Adventures at Aurora, $8.95 paper.
___Copy(ies) Mark Twain: His Life In Virginia City, Nevada, $10.95 paper.
___Copy(ies) Mark Twain and the Jumping Frog, $8.95 pap.
___Copy(ies) On the Road with Mark Twain In California and Nevada, $16.95 paper; $29.95 Library Hardcover.
___Copy(ies) The Songwriter's Demo Manual, $29.95.
___Copy(ies) Repair Your Credit, $16.95

Shipping by postal service is $2.25 for the first book, $1 each additional book. Faster shipping via Priority Mail is $3.95 for the first book $1.00 each additional book.

Total for books_____
Shipping _____
Total enclosed in check or money order ________
Mail your order to:

TBR Trust
P.O. Box 20703-CL
Carson City, Nevada 89721
www.Autographed-Books.com